Welc[illegible] *to the* Light

A Trumpet of Truth

Karl Krahn

Your dreams will come ture, you found your way home

Printed in the United States of America
ISBN: Softcover 978-1-63871-868-0
eBook 978-1-63871-869-7
Republished by: PageTurner Press and Media LLC
Publication Date: 01/07/2022

To order copies of this book, contact:
PageTurner Press and Media
Phone: 1-888-447-9651
info@pageturner.us
www.pageturner.us

CONTENTS

Poet's Bio:

. . . . If you are happy with the way this world has prepared for the second coming of Christ, fine. Go your merry way and enjoy. I am not, and the results are why you are reading this story. I was raised by a very strong believing Mother. She taught the truth always wins, be sure your sins will find you out and as you sow, so shall you reap.

. . . . She didn't prepare me for this world, but for the next. When I finally understood this, it was too late. I could not believe it was possible to have the Spirit of Jesus Christ enter my heart, mind and soul, and feel no difference. For years I searched for the feeling of total acceptance. I often felt the presence of the Holy Spirit, but it was always in someone else. I could not find the feelings, I was looking for. It's not possible to list the extent and searching of this journey, but in the end, I gave up.

. . . . If there is no God, it makes no difference. If there is a God, and He won't talk to me, that's worse. So I quit. The last day, when al living beings go before the final judgement, I have no defense. I believed, by not talking to me, God was not living up to His promise. Then I got very happy.

. . . . All my worries about Hell's fury and roasting for the rest of time, vanished. I set a time limit of three weeks and then I was going to stop living. Nothing fancy, I was going to find a simple way to stop living. I rejected this life completely. My worries were over.

. . . . Then, after two weeks, I got an overwhelming desire to get a pencil and paper. The desire was so strong, if I didn't have paper in time, I would write on table tops or anything that was handy. They were poems. They came pouring from my hand. They came so fast, there is no way I could tell them that fast. Now I offer them to those that think there has to be more in this life.

. . . . The hope and prayers that we will be covered by His Loving Grace, even though we make no effort to live better, just don't wash. If you want to live again, you have got to try. I say again. If you believe you already have a passkey to Heaven, Have a nice day. If these poems can help one person, Praise God!!

Dedication:

Dedicated to the Co-Authors:

God the Father

God the Son

God the Holy Spirit

"May God Bless the hands thar hold this Book"

WAKE UP!!

. . . . I just made such a strong statement, it seems everyone is in shock. How does this lowly human think he has the right to go against today's common thought? What gives him the right to believe he can talk and listen to Jesus and His father, God?

. . . . It's OK for the believers in this earth to think a chosen few get to talk to them. If you give enough to the church, you might even get to go to Heaven. Some even think there is only one way to get to Heaven and that's with the help of a preacher.

. . . . If you search the words God left, in the Bible, you will find at least two meanings For everything written. The "Holy People" have taken control of God's House and written their own rules.

. . . . Most of today's churches have relaxed God's word to the extent, there is no longer a need to repent. They have also convinced themselves that works are a thing of the past. Most quote Paul and believe works is something that no longer has value. In the New Testament, a whole chapter is written about faith and works. The second chapter of James has been completely ignored.

. . . . Now all you have to do, is say you know who Jesus is, fill the offering plate, and don't worry. You now have a passkey to the Gates of Heaven. Today's way of belief is, you don't even have to try. An untold truth, that only the "Holy People" control, will save us all.

. . . . Why don't you use common sense and Something reasoning? Why would God come to this earth, in the form of His Son, give humans the chance to live again, then make it so easy to do? Don't forget. He was killed for spreading love and making the offer of life.

. . . . No, I am not trying to explain all about religion. Religion is a lifetime study of something that no one seems to understand. I am telling you how to meet my friend, Jesus.

"How about trying to Wake Up?"

. . . . God gave His Son to die on the cross so your God can live inside you. It's really very simple. It's one on one. If you now believe that truth over powers evil, then quit evil, ask and Jesus will enter your heart.

. . . . Now that you have met Jesus, you must have good Intentions and be willing to live for goodness. Ask Him in, believe He's there and talk to Him inside yourself. It's God's promise, if you ask, He will enter.

. . . . Okay, you asl Him. Do you think God Would put His Son inside your heart, and make Him mute? Not hardly. Some (most?) people think the voice you hear inside yourself is your conscience. Granted. That is what it is called, so it can be explained.

. . . . After you have Jesus in your heart, you must use His name to talk to His Father. You must ask His Father to put His Son's voice inside you, so you can hear Him. Then believe it. Jesus says in the Bible, "My Sheep Know my Voice." That is where doubt comes in. When you hear the voice of Jesus, you can't doubt it. You must believe. As long as you are seeking Jesus or the voice of Jesus, You are covered by God's Grace. God knows the difference. It is something the devil can't fake.

. . . . I know what the problems of doubt are. Over the years I have doubted many times, but Jesus has always been there for me. When you believe in Jesus and His Father, your problems are not over. They are just beginning. When you live for Jesus, you must also believe, the devil is very real. He will try In every way to spoil your belief. Then you must remember, you are no longer alone.

. . . Even if you can't believe what I say, think about it. Jesus and His Father are waiting to meet you.

THE FANTASY?

. . . . This is note to all the born again Christians. The ones that would really rather give up their present life and turn to the straight and narrow, if they could fine the right way. The ones that have heard all the efforts this world has to offer and have not found their answer. In short, No one has found the true way to explain the fact that God is. This fact has been so covered up by non-believers, the real truth is now thought to be a myth.

. . . (1)—Yes, you did it right. You met Jesus in His Church and invited Him into your heart. It was then explained by the preacher, all your sins are washed away. By the Grace Of God and His Son Jesus Christ, Baptism cleanses all your past sins. The preacher then explains, The Grace from God insures you will sin no more.

Enough said .

But:

. . . . Nobody explained why, when iniquity is questioned, the answer is always the same. Iniquity and sin are the same. God's Grace covers it all. John 3:16 insures that any person that believes that Jesus Christ is the true Son Of God, will have everlasting life. So the modern way of living is to get Jesus in your heart and then do anything you want. After all, you don't have to worry about Hell anymore.

. . . Iniquity is much stronger than sin. When all your sins were forgiven and you no longer had to fear Hell, you entered the realm of Iniquity. In this beautiful realm, you had better look before you leap.

. . . Remember, you now have Jesus Christ in your heart. He has promised to stay with you forever. No force can remove Him. Jesus has joined His spirit to yours. Everything in your life, is now in direct contact with God. Through Jesus in your heart, God has an up close view of every breath you take.

. . . Iniquity is knowing your thoughts are wrong, and doing them anyway. To drag the Spirit of God through the foulest evil you can find, with all the pleasures you can afford, is not forgiven lightly. Maybe this will give you the idea.

. . . When God created this world, He used spirits for building blocks. Including man, everything on the earth has a spirit. Even rocks are alive. It's in the Bible, look it up. Every living thing on this earth, has a spirit. God has promised all people that believe in His Son, a new earth.

. . . Where in the world is God going to find building spirit blocks that will be pure enough to build the foundations of our new world. There is a complete supply just waiting to be used. Every spirit in the block pile is half the spirit of Jesus. That's the reason they were given everlasting life. God would not send any part of His Son Jesus to hell.

. . . "As you sow-so shall you reap". This statement decides your lasting position on this new World. If God shows no mercy because of what you made His Son suffer through, it's His choice. Just think, there's a very large possibility you will spend forever everlasting as a spirit locked in a rock. As for all the Christian mothers that aborted their babies for personal reasons. They may find they are now in the body of a penguin, holding their eggs on top of their feet to keep them from freezing. The possibility's are endless. Forever everlasting is a long, long time

. . . Jesus made very clear instructions on how His believers were to conduct themselves. In the New Testament He went to great lengths to explain at a sermon that was later called, the Sermon on the Mount. Impossible you ask? With help from God, nothing is impossible.

. . . This item was not written to amuse anyone. If you think this is all a bunch of crazy talk, relax. See you on the rock pile.

BEWARE

If only my casket had windows.
If I had the power to see;
I'd take a quick look toward Heaven,
and enter my final plea.

O Lord, You know I'm a sinner.
Have mercy, O Lord, on me.
I seem to be a forgotten son,
this casket has no Key.

It seemed an answer would not come,
but much to my surprise;
this thought came flashing to my mind,
"It's right before your eyes."

"The Key is where you left it,
just remember if you can;
the person that you loaned it to,
but not a helping hand."

"Remember the girl on crutches,
or the dirty old man in the park?
The one with little enough to eat?
The one with a broken heart?"

"You might ask the man that had it,
as you helped him on the road;
by showing him a shorter path;
but carried not his load."

"The Key was offered many times,
in trials of the past;
the place you have to find it,
is the place you left it last."

"Truth and Love and Charity,
will bring you home to me;
but first you must repent your sin,
for Jesus is the Key."

So listen very closely,
to this story that I tell;
Without the Key of Life, my friend,
Your destination's Hell.

THE GIVEN LIGHT

The light that shines through Heaven's door
is pure in every way.
It's not confused by reason
or the things some people say.

To stand in light so pure and bright,
is everybody's dreams;
But all that try to please themselves,
just don't know what it means.

To give it all, is just a part of giving,
don't you see?
For Jesus gave until He died,
He did not think of "Me".

With Grace from God and all that's true,
we'll have a great tomorrow;
But those that stop to think of "Me",
will find they have much sorrow.

As you sow, so shall you reap,
is God's most given right.
Just trust in Him, and try your best,
you'll see His precious light.
To help the poor and those that need,
will bring you much, and more.
Your helping will insure a place,
inside of Heaven's door.

THE REPLY

There once was a boy
that wanted to see,
the world by and large
from the top of a tree.

He climbed all the way
to the limbs that were small,
he couldn't climb higher,
for fear of a fall.

"Father?" he asked
as he started back down,
"Know a way here on earth
to make those limbs sound?"

"Son," he replied
with a tear in his eye,
"if you push God to far,
you surely will die."

"The top, as you know,
is made of limbs smaller.
To balance the rest,
so it can grow taller."

"Created for man,
both the old and the young,
the trees are a blessing,
a song to be sung."

"For a man to view
the sights from above;
he must give of his all,
and his all must be love."

"The people that try
to climb to the top,
just find on their way,
there's no place to stop."

"The top, it stays limber
and bends to the ground,
the bottom is up
and the up part is down."

"The view from the top
is not worth it, you see?
It's all upside down
and it's all misery."

"The higher a man
can climb in his eyes,
is his sight from down under,
the moment he dies."

"So stay on the ground
and view trees with care,
when we go with Jesus,
we'll see from up there."

SOFT TOUCH

The common word for devils help
is luck, don't you agree?
Good luck is getting, right on time,
the things you want to see.

But when you know your help is coming,
from the Lord above;
It's not the devil's luck at all,
but portions of God's love.

To pray and ask for others,
all the things you know they need;
but brag not when it happens,
God has planted you as seed.

Praying is man's best defense,

from trouble and from strife;
Planting love is growing shown,
on this tall tree of life.

Believe in Jesus,
then you'll see,
your problems will increase.
For satan's trying with his might,
to make your praying cease.

When he causes doubt and fear,
the devil knows he's winning;
and if he can, he'll try his best,
to make you think you're sinning.
Want and greed is all he needs,
to show his earthly power;
when you pray and give your love,
you're in your finest hour.

Jesus knows the times are bad,
the ones you're going through;
He gave us love and showed the way,
His grace and love are true.

Seven come eleven is the devil's
prayer for certain;
to hang before man's greedy face,
his earthly power curtain.

So when you hear someone rejoice
at making lucky seven;
just say you'll wait to have your luck,
the day you get to Heaven.

THE REASON

Heaven has no keep out signs,
it's free in every way.
It's free of gossip making
and the fear of what you say.

The vain were sorted, long ago
and liars were laid to rest;
thieves had stolen their own soul
and failed the final test.

No pretending felt or shown
on streets of solid gold;
A place where smiles are love itself,
a place you don't get old.

And there in Heaven, it's a joy,
to praise and give a nod;
And thank the reason you are there,
the Holy Son Of God.

UNTOLD TRUTH?

Is there a truth that can't be told?
A question asked by young and old.
But times have dimmed without a care,
don't be surprised if lies we share.

An honored man, a man of God,
that hears a lie, then gives a nod;
Is doing more than planting fear,
For God above, is standing near.

He thinks his God has made it law,
an untold truth will save us all;
A saying he can always win,
I know the Lord, I have no sin.

Your sins are gone, all washed away,
when Jesus comes inside to stay.
Your sin has gone, is true to say,
Iniquity, now has its day.

Look to the Lord, for He has said,
Iniquity, is hell unread.
A knowing sin is all it takes,
a devil's hug, your souls at stake.

For every breath we take, we share.
You are the one that asked Him there;
to force our Lord to sin and lust,
inside our heart, is black and rust.

Enjoy His love and wake to fact,
read your Bible and love Him back.
Then pray to God, and live to try,
An untold truth, is an untold lie.

A ROSE

If man could tell the beauty, of a rose.
Without the cunning senses, of his nose.
He would notice, first of all,
petals come and petals fall;
The beauty comes from nothing, then it goes.

To enjoy the precious story, they could tell.
Of three long days that Jesus, spent in Hell.
You must first enjoy the feeling,
When He went, that He was knelling;
For the Grace of God, His Father, taught Him well.

The color is the center, of His heart.
He knew the test was coming, from the start.
Now, the devil tried to say,
You will suffer most today;
But he didn't know that God was there in part.

Then the devil made his move, to take command.
He tried his very best, to break the man.
But Dear Jesus put His trust,
And He found this part a must;
In the morning, He would see the promised land.

Then the devil lost his power, don't you see?
Tho the rulers of the darkness, danced in glee.
What they really didn't know,
Was that God, who loved Him so;
Had entrusted Him with knowledge, and the Key.

So remember as you live, for me and mine.
You are letting Jesus die, upon the vine.
Give your love to Dad and Mother,
Trust in Jesus and no other;
Then the beauty of the rose, will come in time.

The Honor of His death, is plain to say.
Every man will hear the trumpet, on his day.
If you live, as He has shown,
Grace from Jesus will be known;
But to seek and find the glory, you must pray.

The tree of life is hollow, as it grows.
The blood of Jesus fills it, as it flows.
The Grace from God is pure,
You will find as you endure;
From the sin and shame of Satan, He A Rose.

NITTY GRITTY

To withdraw from Bible teaching
when you hear His chosen preaching;
is the crime of people lost,
that know the way.

Just don't think to get to Heaven
you can throw a lucky seven;
cause on judgment day,
the truth will have its say.

Tho you just can't seem to buy it
and to scared of death to try it;
here and now's the time and place,
to lose the devil.

It's not what you must fear
that brings the Lord so near;
It's truth to tell,
if you are on the level.

The choice that God has given
to this world of fancy livin,
is a life to live again,
in time to come.

Jesus loved and helped the others
but some people have their druthers;
and the race they do not try,
can not be won.

So put down your liquor drinking
for it has your breath a stinking,
and enjoy no more your thrill,
of nasty habits.

All your rolling in the clover
and your fancy body odor;
is offending to the name,
of nature's rabbits.

No one's perfect you will say
as the devil has his day;
many tried and many failed,
or so I'm told.

You can quit your Bible pounding
for the devils you are drowning;
are the ones you always get,
when you are old.

But the eyes were made for seeing
and to see the devil fleeing;
is a joy for all the righteous,
and the true.

If it's on your toes I'm trodding
it's the truth that needs a prodding,
for this message, it was written,
just for you.

DO YOU HEAR?

I just don't want to hear it,
is the phrase most people say;
if I know not what I'm doing,
I'll get by on judgment day.

I just don't want to hear it,
is the devils battle hymn;
he try's to be so righteous,
but his middle name is sin.

Sometimes he makes you wonder,
with his money and his might;
if the Lord has done him dirty,
if he's really in the right.

But in truth, there is no question,
for he lies and steals and cheats;
It is from the blood of others,
that he gets the love he eats.

So depend on love from Jesus
and rely on Him alone.
You can trust the Son of God to be,
the friend that's always home.

CHANCY

If your soul was in your palm,
beneath the skin.
Would you worry where to put it,
when you sin?

Would you ask the Lord to hold it,
then come back and say He stole it;
being careful cause you know
the mood He's in?

Or would you run and hide,
with the devil keeping stride;
and relax your grip a little,
now and then?

And just knowing that it's chancy,
wear a glove that's clean and fancy;
then convince yourself with mercy,
I can win?

When the trumpet sounds for glory,
and your hands are blood and gory;
there's no time to get them clean,
or even pray.

Knowing well, the straight and narrow,
you will blame the other fellow;
when the time has come to face,
your judgment day.

While you're still among the living,
and the Good Lord still is giving;
now's the time to have Him wash it,
with His word.

For your soul just will not make it,
if you let the devil take it;
and then try to tell the Lord,
you haven't heard

DREAM DAZE

At the edge of creation, all covered with mist;
is a kingdom of love, that time must have missed.
A land of such beauty, where all have the right;
to see golden rainbows, of misty delight.

Time has not settled, or quickened its pace;
to find such a land, in this beautiful place.
A land of such beauty and meanings of bliss.
A land that is governed by true happiness.

Balanced by thought, at the edge of a stream;
this kingdom of love, is like living a dream.
A dream of such color, that sharpens the mind;
the shades are not faded, though efforts of time.

An empire of floral, that's floating in foam;
the dream of tomorrow, the kingdom calls home.
Floating on pads, that are anchored in place;
by strands of the timeless, of strength and of grace.

To enter this kingdom, just follow your heart.
You'll never know, when the journey will start.
It might happen quickly, you might be alone;
Your dreams all come true, you're on your way home.

HONOR

It's something you don't brag about,
or lightly use in jest.
It used to be a word of pride,
but now it's just a test.

It seems to be forgotten grace
from friends so long ago;
their word and one small handshake,
would strike a legal blow.

But now that trust has fallen prey
and truth a twisted lie;
It makes you wonder where it went,
this love of days gone by.

So mellow out, save your breath
and watch this world at play;
they'll find out what honor is,
the coming judgment day.

Monkey's Uncle?

It really makes you wonder
what the teachers say today.
Where do they get the reason
for confusing things they say?

They teach the fact of life to all
and prove without a doubt;
that monkeys are relation,
their creation helped us out.

They have opposing fingers
and the way their head is shaped;
against all bible teachings,
they still say we come from apes.

But questions rise before our eyes,
when did their life begin?
For God condemned whole tribes for sin,
Did monkeys come from men?

LOVE'S MELODY

Real love can't be described in words,
but listen closely to the birds.
Some try, but have no voice at all,
for some just quack and others caw.

But birds that sing of Jesus love,
are birds of blessing from above.
They sing to Jesus every day,
in words us mortals can not say.

The songs they sing have different sounds,
and listen how their love abounds.
For never has a note been heard,
that was not perfect from a bird.

They grumble when it's raining hard,
or even quarrel when they're tired.
But when they sing in notes so true,
just listen as they talk to you.

For Jesus lives inside us all,
He's waiting for your need and call.
Remember when you hear birds sing,
It's God, He's offering everything.

MOTHER'S SOUP

Once, when I was just a boy,
my Mother made it plain;
No matter what you do in life,
bring Honor to your name.

To lie and cheat is easy,
but a time will always tell;
The day of final judgment,
It will get you sent to Hell.

A place where boiling supper,
is served in flaming bowls;
and glowing right beside them,
is the lying cheating souls.

We both know, you'll try your best,
to make me out a liar;
but you will find, no peace of mind,
when your butt's on fire.

The only way to warn a liar,
is catch him in the act;
then prove beyond all reason,
that now, his lie, is fact.

And as to all your cheating,
it counts double, don't you see?
Cause you must lie, to cause a cheat,
and then remember me.

I wish that you would listen,
and I hope you even try;
to live your life with honor,
at the judgment, you'll know why.

So take this as a warning,
you will reap just what you sow;
and don't complain about the soup,
just have another bowl.

TO QUESTION

Is beauty in a lifeless stone
the image of a heart alone?
Or is it something you must feel
to see the things you think are real?
A Wonder.

Is what the artist had to say,
still life, that's living for a day?
Or is it something from within,
that lives inside the hearts of men?
A Wonder.

To ask is human and a form
of wonder for the things we mourn,
But is the portion we can see,
the life we form from memory?
A Wonder.

Cause even when all mankind knows;
it's not the question that he shows;
But in his heart it's what he sees,
that Jesus loves both you and me.
A Wonder.

For Jesus died upon the cross,
to show us truth, we had not lost.
It was His way to show us love,
from God forgotten from above.
A Wonder.

A sample of His caring touch,
He left to show, He loves you much;
by all the life that's on the earth,
the birds and such that knows His worth.
A Wonder.

For beauty has as beauty is,
God shows His love, to what is His.
A wonder is a precious right,
just knowing you are in His sight.
A Wonder.

CHRISTIAN HARVEST

Daily life is like a painting,
every picture has its say.
Stored together for the showing
brought to life on judgment day.

Hope is mixed with every color,
mixed with love and tender care.
Every deed is shown in motion,
every smile and every prayer.

Evening mist is highly favored,
showing Grace from God above;
It's His way to show His Blessing,
to His Son that shares His love.

Painting daily takes an effort,
keeping colors blended light;
If mistakes are sometimes handy,
Jesus loves to make them right.

Brush the strokes with lightened shadows,
cast of gold to darkened brown;
Smiles of light with happy colors,
dimming to a cheerful frown.

Told of riches beyond reason,
happy now you're soon to be;
Open now your eyes for glory,
open wide for all to see.

Relax, enjoy and rest your spirit,
reap the harvest you have grown;
Now's the time to count your blessings,
now you meet the love you've sown.

THE SEED

People that crave all the thrills of this life,
will do anything, for the money;
Like a bear sure enough, with hunger and wants,
will die for a jar, full of honey.

Said the men of old, the men that had wisdom,
that lived so long ago;
This life is not over, It's not even started,
It's but a seed we sow.

If the seed has a portion of all that is lovely,
the righteous who plant it, will weep;
For bad is the taste, of the fruit of this life,
if the seed we don't plant it, we eat.

So remember the bear and try if you will,
to open your eyes, just a moment;
This life is the jar, or the seed that we plant, the
honey we crave, but don't own it.

PASS-KEY

Religion is a study of
the things man wants to see;
If it don't interfere with life,
and leaves the rest to me.

The churches teach and show the way,
to see God's Holy Face.
They change the rules to meet their needs,
depending on God's Grace.

Some even say, you sin no more,
for they have ways to know;
Their Grace from God is pass-key true,
to Heaven you will go.

Most teach to know of Jesus Christ,
is all you have to do;
But ask the question to yourself,
does Jesus Christ know you?

Remember this and seek His love,
to give to those that hate;
For Jesus is the only key,
that opens Heaven's Gate.

TWISTED WISDOM

As it is written, without any doubt,
A Savior was sent, to seek the good out.
To help in the process, a statement was shown,
If you love the Savior, He'll build you a home.

A home that is flawless, of jewels and gold,
A land that is pure, where you never grow old.
The few that can differ, they try to live right,
Will be loved forever, with His righteous might.

But life is a puzzle that does let you down,
Do you hate with a smile, or love with a frown?
The words God told His Wise Men to write,
He told of His mercy, He told of His bite.

But man has decided in moments of glee,
He meant them for you, He didn't mean me.
The right was shown white, and the wrong colored black,
The line was drawn heavy, not shaded or slack.

Men have shown weakness and taught us to say,
We can't make wrong white, so we'll color it gray.
But look as you can and seek as you must,
God never said gray was a color to trust.

Man changed the meaning of love that is gay,
To mean things forbidden, a cool thing today.
Or cheating to cover our corporate greed,
We won't see the wrong if it covers our need.

Questions arise when wrong has it's say,
What color is white, if we shade it with gray?
Some people must twist, they must criticize,
They won't admit truth, in front of their eyes

But they'll see the truth, be judged when they die,
You can't hide the truth, though many will try.
His sermon shows guidance, the one on the mount,
His words are pure white, on that you can count.

WORTH?

It's time to listen, hear it loud,
and try to read my lips;
The game of life is ending,
and it's time to count your chips.

If you can touch your values
and the feel is clammy cold;
It's time to rearrange your thoughts,
and feed your starving soul.

If all you crave, is me and mine,
your focus all on me;
Please follow for a moment's flash
and try your best to see.

The only things of value
that will make your soul complete;
Are mixed with love and sharing,
as you sow, so shall you reap.

So gather all your loving seeds
and plant them every day;
The love that feeds your hungry soul
is love you give away.

While you're gathering up your chips
and counting what you've won;
Your precious soul is all that's left,
until the game is done.

So if you want to live again,
be careful what you say;
The counting starts the day you die,
and lasts till judgment day.

EFFORT

The many times you try your best,
you find without a doubt;
Someone that sees your effort,
will come by and help you out.

These words were taught to children,
they were told of Heaven's dreams;
When God could teach the masses,
what He says is what He means.

Like loving one another,
even though it's hard to do;
The kind of love that listens,
even when they don't love you.

Like living truth with honor,
daring not to tell a lie;
Being scorned by many watchers,
who have lost the will to try.

Truth and trust are all but gone,
and no one saw them go;
The lies and cheats are everywhere
and no one tells them no.

Listen now and understand,
true love is meant to mend;
Friendship is not taken free
for you must earn a friend.

So open up your heart a bit,
with hope of being heard;
The loving best a man can be,
is when he keeps his word.

THINK!!

The young that want to get ahead
on this tall tree of life;
will find the limbs are far apart,
and slimed with grief and strife.

To climb the ladder that's nearby,
that's made by all your friends;
they smile and offer both their hands,
and help that never ends.

But those that hurry beyond help
and think of only me;
will stomp the heads of everyone
and climb to victory.

The ladder is the climb of choice,
the stairway's not complete;
the stay on top is sometimes short,
the fall is very steep.

But grab the ladder coming down,
and bless those helping hands;
they catch and slow the mighty fall
and soften where you land.

But you will miss the rungs you stomped,
the heads you used by force;
those rungs will cause an awful fall,
cause they'll be gone, of course.

So think about rewards you lose,
when falling to your grave;
It's not about the toys you won,
but love you gave away.

TRIAL QUESTION

If wrong and right was brought to light
and judged for all to see;
which side would win, then win again,
if wrong was misery.

It seems the line, that is so fine,
if drawn as God has taught;
The wrong would be, for all to see,
the loser lost and caught.

When I was raised and Christ was praised,
my Mother taught me well.
She taught me doubt would find you out,
and sinners went to hell.

But now it seems, with twisted dreams,
that truth is just a myth;
If you can show a doubt to know,
the truth is used to twist.

But right is there for those that care
and those that really try;
For Jesus gave, so He could save,
or did my Mother lie?

THE FOOL

Said a man one day
as he tried to play,
with a toy that would not start.
This God damn thing
means I can't bring,
a smile into my heart.

I'll try one time,
invest one dime
and then I'll ask the Lord;
To lend a hand,
to help this man,
to swing His heavy sword.

As you can guess,
he'd brought duress
upon his life for sure;
His toy was jammed,
as he had damned,
God gives a love that's pure.

THE VICIOUS SISTERS

To meet them you would laugh out loud,
the story's they can tell;
of all the people they have met,
that's headed straight to hell

To hear the love they gave away,
and suffering they've endured
it's best if you just turn away,
and question what you've heard.

They sing and shout and jump about,
on Sundays, it's their way;
to show and brag to others,
their rewards on judgment day.

To live the way they want,
is their story, tried and true;
and if you question any part,
it's straight to hell with you.

To spread their lies and gossip,
over forty years of time;
to ruin many memories,
a secret, yours or mine?

They can't seem to harbor,
any truth they hear from you;
if you try to beg for mercy,
for the crime you didn't do.

They claim their christian values,
that are pure in every way;
the Blood of Christ they're covered with,
won't pass the DNA.

So when you see them all in church,
all acting sweet, like cupid;
the names that match their way of life,
are Renie, Mutt and Stupid.

Be careful of the things you hear,
what God has planned to do;
and ask the Christians that you meet,
"Does Jesus Christ know you?

IGNORING GOD?

A carefully planned effort on God's part,
has failed again. Someone must be listening,
for His efforts to be heard. Over the last 100
Years, God has tried countless times to get
The attention of His believers. Though no one
seemed to notice;

There was an earthquake in San Francisco.
No response.

Two freak airplane wrecks occurred that
caused both pilot's cabin to be
Completely torn off both planes. One in the east and
One in the west. Something to joke about.
No response.

New Orleans was soaked with a try for
attention but many were saved, only
because of the masses crying out to God
for help. Their own country would not
help them.
No response.

Hostages were taken and held 444 days
as foretold in the Bible. In the same time
period, the whole top blew off Mt. Saint
Helen, as foretold in the Bible.
No Response.

The day the towers fell, Many cries were
heard and many approached God asking
for revenge. No public words were said,
asking for God's reason. The falling towers
were foretold, in the Bible.
No Response.

The only time, man has been brought to
his knees, in this great land of freedom,
was the dust bowl. The people finally
realized, God is in control.

God left some signs that blank out the Big Bang theory. Have you ever looked at a flat globe map? Do it. If you don't see the pictures, God left as a sign, you must be spiritually blind. Check out the giant prehistoric bird of prey. And while you're at it, check out the giant dragon. One's carrying a large hive and the other is eating from a large honey nest. Imagination? God don't think so.

It's time to wake up, Christians, or God will really get your attention.

GOD'S LAST WARNING?

Before anyone big or small can be held accountable, first they must be accused. In the name of God and His Son, Jesus Christ, I Accuse.

God's Last Warning?

The United States has fought many countries for acts of inhuman actions against their own people. Humans are supposed to have certain rights, under God, that can not be denied.

. . . . Now it is time to expose a monster crime, against our own people. It has been reported, since 1973 there has been 60 million babies aborted in the name of free rights. Women have the right to abort any baby that is not wanted. Murder.

. . . The excuse used to justify this mass murder?
Life don't start until the baby is developed
to a certain stage. They state the baby does
not have a soul until a certain time. The main theme
in their story? When does life start?

. . . . If this question was asked in any part of the
world but ours, they would laugh.

. . . . Life does not start. It continues.

. . . . If Hitler killed less than ten million, and
he has been declared as the filth of time,
what does that make us? So far this nation
has killed over sixty million and counting.

. . . . If these facts are not given to the people, they will not know why God has condemned this country. Already, earth quakes and other attempts from God to get our attention has failed. Thousands of dead birds falling from the sky, didn't even rate the front page, more than once. No one cares.

. . . . Remember the cities God deleted? He did it with fire and ash. The last time God managed to get the attention of this country, He did it with a dust bowl.

I-RAN?

Before anyone big or small can be held accountable, first they must be accused. In the name of God and His Son, Jesus Christ, I Accuse.

It's not a Holy War.

I-Ran?

. . . . The first time this nation had dealings with a Country named Iran, they were in a power struggle. We had just learned, their country was sitting on the biggest oil reserve in the World. We chose a side, gave them money and guns, and watched the show.

. . . . The Shah won. He took the guns we gave him and lined a hundred thousand souls against the wall, and fired. The war was won and we now had an unlimited oil supply. We gave the Shah so much money, it was cheaper to give him a money press than ship him money. And we did. We gave him, his own, money printing press.

. . . . The Shah used his new found wealth to buy super prime property all over the world. Billions of dollars were spent in this country alone and the value just kept getting bigger.

. . . . He did not share his wealth with any of his people. They were mostly poor and just barely getting by. They still fought for their rights and were still being killed.

. . . . When the injured party, of Iran, finally got strong enough to threaten the Shah, he ran. Taking all he could carry, he left the country to live elsewhere. Sick, unwelcome and sadly rejected from every country he ask, he finally was admitted entry into the U.S.A., claiming he had cancer. He was right.
He died.

. . . . The new leaders of Iran asked the U.S.A. to give them their money back. After all the Red Tape was thrown at them, the answer was no.

. . . . Iran then took all the Americans that were
at the U.S. Embassy and held them as a way,
to show token resistance. Answer? No.
We Will not pay for Hostages.

. . . . Acting the part of a playground bully, the U.S.A.
decided to take the Hostages by force. They
sent a secret convoy of armed choppers with
a cargo of our best fighters, to save the Hostages.
The plan was to enter across their northern
deserts and hope for no contest. Wrong.

. . . . God was the contest. Where the freak sand
storm came from is a total mystery. Choppers
ran into each other and lives were lost.
The plan was aborted.

. . . . Know how many days the Hostages were held?
As God foretold over two thousand years ago, they
were held 444 days. He also forecast the top
would blow off the tremulous ones. In the
same time frame, a whole cubed mile blew
off the top of Mt. St. Helen.

. . . . It's in the Bible. Look it up.

. . . . Because of our history, God has taken His Blessings from this country and bestowed them on the small Country of Iran. If we make moves of any kind, to hurt or injure Iran, we will waken the wrath of God.

. . . . Where are all God's Christians? Most churches are bragging about knowing Jesus and go to great length to take care of God's money. The Bible is filled with stories of the POWER of GOD. In times past, He has used that Power because one real Christian ask Him.

. . . . But first it's time to find a real live Man of God, that cares to ask Him.

. . . . In years gone by, the symbol that graced this country was a shiny pure white hat. Now this symbol of slime has reduced it's self to the same wreath the Romans used to wear. Only this wreath is made from a Ball of serpents, all biting themselves.
. . . . Repent.

"LIVING LOVE"

. . . . As cross country truck driver, and a person that depends on certain events to always have a margin of chance, I try to live in the extreme present… . Murphy's law, if it can happen, it will, is the law of survival.

. . . . Once in a while, when you least expect it, something happens that throws your whole world into a second by second picture. You can never forget.

. . . . All my days I have read and heard people try to explain, in words, the meaning of love. It's a whole lot like trouble. You're either in trouble or you're not. It's the very same thing about love. You know, you're either in love or you're not in love. No one can tell you, you just know.

. . . . On a return trip from Phoenix to El Paso, I was very tired an sleepy. When I got close to Tucson, I pulled into the Triple "T" truck stop. A good meal would perk me right up. I parked, shut down and headed for the diner.

. . . . As I crossed the lobby, it happened. Three people were coming out of the double glass doors to the diner. There was a man about forty, a lady about the same age, his wife? and a much older man. This is the one that got my attention.

. . . . He was so bent over at the waist, it was amazing he could even stand. He was bent over so far, he had to throw his head all the way back, just to see the floor. As the younger man held the door, the old man shuffled though.

Everyone in the lobby suddenly went to alert. A strong feeling of shame mixed with fear, had swept the lobby. It was so strong, everyone looked away.

. . . . Standing close and feeling so totally helpless,
all I could manage was a very weak, “Hello”.
He shuffled around sideways, turned his head to the left,
and in a frightened voice said “Hi”.
The younger couple was standing behind him,
heads hung low, as if wanting to go unnoticed.
There was no sound at all in the lobby.
No one moved.

. . . . Then the spell was broken. A tall gray
haired lady came in from the diner and
was explaining why she took so long. The
credit card thing was down and she had
to pay cash.

. . . . As she approached the old man, she seemed
to grow smaller. She bent all the way over
to his stance, took his offered hand
in hers and as her eyes came into his focus,
she asked, “You OK?”
In a strong voice he answered,
“I am now.”

. . . . Together, in his world, I watched them
shuffle away.

COLOR-FAST

Ask me why my shoes don't match,
I say to all I meet.
The story is a blessing taught,
to souls with searching feet.

While walking in a park called Ropes,
on Corpus Christi bay;
we wandered to the shoreline sand,
one bright and sunny day.

My wife and I were talking
of the life that is to come,
and all the blessings we'll receive,
when triumphs we have won.

I happened once to mention,
why I seemed to have the blues,
cause on my feet I'm wearing,
just a worn out pair of shoes.

Knowing that God heard me,
was a feeling of delight.
For lying up the beach a ways,
a shoe had caught my sight.

Just exactly like the ones
that I have always worn,
But this was new, the color to,
and this one was not torn.

We searched to find the matching mate,
we tried with all our might.
The one we sought was for the left,
for now we had the right.

In truth, it was a blessing
I was seeking from above;
the proof that He is watching,
with His tenderness and love.

Our car is small and what we have,
is much compared to size.
For we must move it all up front,
so we can rest our eyes.

We clean it out, about the first
of every living day;
for we have nothing but our love,
and money we can save.

My wife is careful, in her way,
of saving all my wants,
When I growled a time or two,
she knew that I was taunt.

A week went by, and soon
I tired of packing every night;
the shoe that God had given,
that was only for the right.

Just trying to relax was hard,
the devil had his say.
I finally gave in to my fears,
and threw the shoe away.

Still looking, with a grain of hope,
to see if I could find,
the proof and shoe that's for the left,
was still upon my mind.

While walking on a beach today,
I found a shoe that fit.
The color matched but it was worn,
I knew it wasn't it.

O Lord, I prayed, if you're still there,
have mercy on me please;
If I deserve a shoe that's worn,
I'll get down on my knees.

Wonder of all wonders,
is the feeling that I felt.
For I could see, the mate for me,
as in my mind I knelt.

Down the beach a little way,
was lying bright and blue,
a shoe the size, with color to,
a left shoe that was new.

O Lord, I'm sorry that I failed
to trust you all the way.
I have feared and thrown away,
the mate the other day.

Disappointment left a taste
of bitter in my heart;
And trusting not with all my soul,
the pain I felt was sharp.

I wandered on along the beach,
self-pity had me now.
I wanted back in God's good Grace,
but could not figure how.

I started once to call it quits,
and live with my dismay.
But thoughts kept coming to my mind,
let Jesus have His say.

I'll trust, I thought with little hope,
to see if I can feel.
God's love so great, He can forgive,
mistakes that are so real.

So on I walked and prayed and talked,
while in a tender state.
But then I gasped and thanked the Lord,
for yonder lay the mate.

The size and color were exact,
the maker was the same.
But this ones not so pretty,
for the sun has done it's thing.

The weather and the time of loss,
it spent upon the beach,
has caused the pretty colors,
to have the cast of bleach.

Now I wear with humble pride,
the shoes God gave to me;
That He both loves and truly cares,
it is no mystery.

DELAYED TRUST

O Lord, you know I love you so
and thank you for your time.
Without your help and by myself,
I'm sure, I'd have lost my mind.

It started on a Monday
as the wind was blowing hard;
We went to Pardre Island,
from this life we are so tired.

The hustle and the rumble
of this modern life is tough;
A day away and we could feel
that livings not so rough.

As we were resting from the trip,
enjoying chosen view;
My wife and I stopped long enough,
to thank and think of you.

Many folks don't stop and see
the things we have been given;
Just laying on their modern beds
and dream of fancy livin.

We noticed in the waste that lay
from Sunday's fun and outing;
Some rope was left along the shore,
it's use there was no doubting.

Since we believe the uses come
for things you care to give;
We gathered up the rope with care,
for that's the way we live.

The tangles were real tight in spots,
with want and bended knee;
We shook them loose and pried the knots,
until they'd all come free.

A joy I have, to pass the time,
one left from navy life;
Is finding rope that's not to worn,
to see if I can splice.

A piece about 10 feet or more
was perfect in it's lenght;
Made of fibers strong and true,
was plentiful in strength.

An eyes not hard, with time and test,
I finally got it done;
This end it felt so good to do,
I did the other one.

When finished, it had quite a look,
this knot that I could tie;
With pleasure I had spliced it right,
but now I wondered why.

A line with loops in both its ends
is different, so it seems;
I put it in the car with care,
still wondering what it means.

Its reason was a puzzle
cause a purpose it must have;
I felt to know the answer
was to feel your healing salve.

Like all of life's small wonders
as we ventured on in time;
We thought of you and what to do,
with this small piece of line.

Come Thursday and a morning
of both troubles and despair;
It rained and though we tried to see,
it seemed you weren't there.

We left the park in search of food
and place to wash and clean;
It was with haste and much regret,
the mud hole wasn't seen.

The car was stuck in such a way,
I know it's seldom done;
The mud was slick and in my mood,
you know it was no fun.

The road nearby was busy
so I hoped against all hope;
We'd finally found the answer
to the double ended rope.

The man that stopped was very nice
and had a brand new truck;
I told him I had problems
and showed him I was stuck.

"Be glad to help" was what he said
"this truck will pull a mile";
"If you've got something we can use",
and then he saw my smile.

We're very thankful for your help
and people that you send;
You've shown us you've not gone away,
You're with us to the end.

The problem you had seen ahead
and gave us love and trust;
Yes Lord, we thank you for the rope,
Among the other stuff.

"AN ODE TO LONESOME JACK"

In a far off draw on a ledge of black,
In a desert so hot it was called out back,
In a kingdom of sorts that was just a shack;
lived a man of rags, called Lonesome Jack;

Quiet and shy with a permanent squint,
He walked in shadows where ever he went,
Blessed the air with his terrible scent;
But a warning he gave, was a warning he meant.

A lifetime friend he had never had,
Most just thought it's because he's bad,
His life was bitter and very sad;
He'd given his love to a world gone mad.

He'd lost his dad in a foreign war,
No way of knowing what the fight was for,
Just kept on loving with a dream for more;
Freedom and peace was the final score.

He walked the streets with his head held high,
Proud of his country but he didn't know why,
To young to vote but not to die;
When the draft board called, he was willing to try.

He was sent to a land beyond the sea,
Where he learned to kill for victory,
Said my friends are dead but why not me?
Now his dreams are hate and misery.

He came back home to begin again,
The dreams were worse, he'd lost his grin,
He ask for help for the shape he was in;
But they sent him to church to repent his sin.

I guess it was then that Jack first cracked,
It was their damned war that he had backed,
It was not his fault their terms had lacked;
So he moved his hell to a run down shack.

Hell's not right, it's a word we use,
To understand hell you have to give up booze,
When Jack first drank, he drank to lose;
Then heat and the desert gave Jack the news.

Bad dreams and hate had left him lame,
He'd tried and failed their pitiful game,
He lived alone to bear their shame;
As the world gave him, he'd give the same.

Out back hot where the birds don't fly,
Where you guzzle your drink, but swallow it dry,
Where sweat don't show and you wonder why;
This out back hot won't let you cry.

His story is told from here to there,
How he grew a long beard and long white hair,
How he carried a gun like a deadly flare;
But his knife was hid, you couldn't see where.

He's not been seen for a long long time,
Some think he died in a caved in mine,
But I toast Ole Jack with a glass of wine;
Cause the hell he left had a vacant sign.

I moved today to his desert shack,
To toast my toes in hell's own crack,
He won't mind cause he won't be back;
His friends came by and he followed their track.

I found a note on Ole Jack's wall,
That damned near made this old man bawl,
You called, I went while standing tall;
You lost, I slipped, you let me fall.

So remember Ole Jack as you eat your feast,
The love of this land made Jack a beast,
The rich do care but they care the least;
So remember Ole Jack as you live in peace.

He gave it all, he gave his best,
He got good grades and passed the test,
The moral is, Ole Jack was blessed;
He gave his life, like all the rest.

CPSIA information can be obtained
at www.ICGtesting.com
Printed in the USA
LVHW040527200122
708837LV00002B/123

9 781638 718680